THE JOYS OF BEING A PROFESSOR

My Life in Academia

ANDREW D. COHEN

LUMINARE PRESS

WWW.LUMINAREPRESS.COM

Printed in the United States of America

Illustrations by Ely Sarig

Cover Design: Melissa Lund
Luminare Press
438 Charnelton St., Suite 101
Eugene, OR 97401
www.luminarepress.com

LCCN: 2018959658
ISBN: 978-1-64388-026-6

*This volume is dedicated to
those wonderful colleagues and students who have
contributed to the joys that I have had as a professor.
Many of the joys that I have experienced over my lifetime
are a direct result of these fine people being there for me
in many different ways, at many different times.
It is in part, then, as a tribute to them that I publish
this volume since I would not have experienced many
of my joys had they not been in my life.*

PRAISE FOR *THE JOYS OF BEING A PROFESSOR*

"This book is a fascinating illustration of how Cohen's outstanding, ground-breaking, and generous contribution to scholarship, scholars, and knowledge-seekers at large becomes the meaningful backbone of his joyful human existence. This delightful read is really about giving one's unique gifts to others unconditionally, and receiving acknowledgement, gratitude, and pleasure in return."

—**GISSI SARIG,** Retired Professor, Kibbutzim College,
now at the Alfred Adler Institution, Israel

"Andrew Cohen captures the joys of being a professor in such a touching matter that it almost makes me wish I hadn't retired. Life in academia indeed offers a rich, rewarding experience, which often continues after one leaves the classroom. Cohen's memoir will bring smiles and wonderful memories to those fortunate enough to have been a professor and inspiration to young teachers and scholars embarking on that journey."

—**SALLY SIELOFF MAGNAN,** Professor Emerita,
University of Wisconsin

"I remember the enthusiasm of the young graduate student I first met at a conference at Stanford, and of the colleague with whom I shared so much while he was at the Hebrew University, and am happy that he has continued to enjoy academic life while contributing so much to students and the field."

—**BERNARD SPOLSKY,** Professor Emeritus, Bar-Ilan
University, Israel

CONTENTS

ACKNOWLEDGEMENTS

My deep thanks go to the following colleagues for their contributions to this volume on professorial joys: Joel Levin, Claire Kramsch, Sally Pierce, Shira Koren, Gissi Sarig, Fredricka Stoller, Bernard Spolsky, Rachel Shively, and Jean-Marc Dewaele. I would also like to think the following colleagues for their suggestions of possible joys over 25 years ago when I first thought of the idea and generated a series of bullets that have now been fleshed out many years later: Elana Shohamy, Merrill Swain, and Rebecca Oxford. To all these wonderful people, and to others who have provided me feedback, many thanks. I also acknowledge Ely Sarig, who – as a high school student – did the wonderful illustrations which appear in this book, and which were originally done for a collection of bullet points which was the predecessor for this volume back in 1998. Ely works as a software user interface designer with Google in Israel. Finally, I would like to acknowledge my wife Sabina for her editorial comments. Even though she requested that I not mention her input, in the interest of full disclosure, be it known that she helped me fine-tune my references to the recipients of joy, whether in reference to me personally or to a more generic professor.

ANDREW D. COHEN
Professor Emeritus, University of Minnesota
1555 Lakeside Drive #182, Oakland, CA 94612
email: adcohen@umn.edu

THE RATIONALE FOR THIS VOLUME

When university professors are asked how their work is going, the response may inadvertently focus on the difficulties associated with the profession rather than on the joys. Our son, Daniel, when he was about to enter his senior year at college 20 years ago, commented more than once that all he heard from me were grumblings about being a professor and that he certainly would not want to pursue the career. So, I gave the issue some thought and realized that his point was well taken.

The issues that I tended to engage in discussion about with colleagues and friends – or had heard others indulging in – had been about matters such as the following:

- Colleagues whose problematic behavior contributed to making my professorial act and that of other colleagues more challenging,

- Demands from the dean or department head to teach more courses per semester and spend more hours in the classroom,

- Pressure to teach undergraduates in large classes without teaching assistants (unless there were 50 or more students),

- The demands of university administrative work, which were likely to involve sitting for hours in sometimes fruitless committee work,
- The hardships of trying to conduct research given the growing number of constraints,
- The difficulty of finding time to complete writing projects,
- The difficulty of getting material published (particularly in prestigious venues).

It is likely that these are just a few of the many issues that he heard me grumbling about.

What about the *joys* of being a professor? What, in fact, are some joys that I have had in being a professor? What about the potential joys that those aspiring to become professors might have in store for themselves if they choose this career as their own? And might this information encourage those who have already started in this career path? It occurred to me that it might also provide interesting reading for those who have been professors for many years in that it may prompt them to take stock of the joys that they themselves have encountered along the way.

The result was the following book, with entries categorized according to different aspects of a professor's professional work life based on my own personal experiences, with the addition of a few others that colleagues have suggested to me.

This is essentially a feel-good volume – to demonstrate both to those in the profession and to those others interested in it some of the ways in which being a professor can produce joy – as I have seen in my 46 years of experience in this career.

I set out to make this a generic collection of joys that would apply to any professor at any level of the spectrum. However, colleagues who read through earlier drafts of this collection felt that in many ways it serves more as my own autobiographic testimony of the professorial joys that I have experienced along the way. In other words, the reaction they had to the collection of joys was that there is no assurance that readers would necessarily experience these same joys.

One option then was to eliminate the honors and other types of acknowledgments that befell me in my career which might only apply to a reduced percentage of professors, and especially to elite researchers rather than to most professors who might never benefit from these opportunities. Another was to leave them in, but make it clear that these joys form part of my memoir rather than reflecting those that are an integral part of any professor's career.

After much thought, I decided to leave them in the volume because I have re-crafted this collection to serve less as a how-to book with regard to *the* joys associated with being a professor, and more as a description of those joys that I personally have experienced and continue to experience in my professorial career, now in an enjoyable semi-retirement phase. That means that I now have ample time to write the papers and books that I wish to without the distraction of having to teach and grade papers. I still travel to domestic and international conferences to give talks and workshops as well. In fact, it is my annual invitations to one or more international meetings that motivate me to keep generating new research studies and publications.

In addition, I am continually involved in reviewing papers for publication in journals, book proposals, and books in draft, as well as reviewing candidates for promotion. So, much of my professorial work continues on, minus the teaching which I enjoyed doing but which took up an inordinate amount of time. The downside of not teaching, of course, is that I am not necessarily as informed about topics within my areas of expertise as I was when I needed to give presentations on these topics in my classes. My solution for that problem is to contact my active colleagues and request that they share with me their most recent work, and this strategy has been a highly effective one for me (as I will share below).

Some of the special joys described in this volume are a result of perks that may be associated with the profession, or at least in my career. This includes travel that is paid for by those who invite me. Another perk was in having paid sabbatical leaves. Yet a third huge one was job security through the tenure process. These perks may even seem unfair to those in other professions where such perks do not exist. If someone is anxious to have these kinds of perks, then that would be all the more reason for them to consider making strides to enter the professorial profession. Of course, as budgets become tighter, institutions are looking at ways to reduce the number of tenured faculty – relying on adjunct professors instead – and maybe even restructuring or eliminating sabbatical leaves.

It is also important to point out that some of the joys mentioned in the volume are most likely to accrue to professors at so-called "Research One" institutions, for whom establishing and maintaining national and international visibility, as well as amassing publications, are crucial if they want to remain at the institution. It is fair to say that professors at major research universities may be more likely to experience some of the joys described below than are

Andrew D. Cohen

colleagues in teaching colleges. For this reason, graduate students aspiring to high levels of national and international recognition for their work may wish to find employment in Research One universities.

Unquestionably, the Technology section below is now dated, but the entries included did involve very real joys for me during my career, just as I assume that future technologies will provide many joys for professors looking ahead. So, mention of my sorting out of email issues and the like serve as a testimony to what was, in fact, a source of joy at the time, whereas now it may be seen as either old-fashioned or simply understood to be the case.

While I will largely refer to my own experiences in this volume, at times I will also refer to professors as a generic group, realizing that in reality there is quite a range. I would like to think that many readers will be able to relate to these joys as ones that they have either had themselves, are likely to have in the future, or could bring about in their own careers as a result of this volume's planting the notion in their minds. Whether such joys are teachable or recommendable will remain an open question. In any event, I felt highly motivated to share this collection with a larger readership, given that it appears there is no such book on the market which celebrates the joys that can be accrued from taking on the career of professor.

TEACHING, COACHING, AND COUNSELING STUDENTS

Teaching, coaching, and counseling one or more of my students so that they (and I) really appreciate the contribution.

Especially when teaching undergraduates, I ended up teaching hundreds of students over the course of my career. Often I did not know just how much of an impact my instruction was having on them, and possibly the students with comments on the course evaluation questionnaires were often those who tended to have some criticism or another. Consequently, at times I was left with the impression that my course was less than splendid and that the impact I had had on students was mixed at best. So it was often a source of delight when students, especially a few years later, contacted me to say that my course had had a tremendous impact on them and that they felt deeply indebted to me. It is true that often this was coupled with the request that I write a letter of recommendation for them, but they would not have turned to me if I had not been a significant player in their education.

Coaching usually produced more immediate results. I could see the impact of, for example, helping students sort out terminology so that they really had a handle on it. Especially if the students being coached were my research assistants, coaching them showed up in most satisfying ways, such as having the data collected or a write up being just what I wanted and then some.

As for counseling, it was very gratifying to provide my

students with suggestions for future career work and then watch them profit from this advice. Even when at the time it may have seemed that my counseling was not likely to make a contribution to their lives, in some cases years later I would learn that it did – and in ways that I had not expected possible. Let us call that a delayed joy.

Having my students who started from scratch become experts in an area that I first directed them into and even surpass my expertise in that area.

This is a super joy in that the essence of professing is ultimately to pass it on. I cannot continue to assume all my professorial duties forever, right? I have already reached the point in my career when I have left my last academic venue and am engaging in various professorial activities from my home in Oakland, California. It is fair to say that much to my surprise and joy, retirement actually entails a "refirement" – where I continue to perform many of my academic tasks, continue to give presentations, run workshops, produce publications, review candidates for promotion, vet papers for journals, and so forth. What I have ceased is the daily teaching which is so crucial for students coming up through the university system. All the more reason, then, to have the comfort of knowing that there are others out there who are providing students with solid educational experiences. It is also possible that my students will, in fact, pursue – and even go beyond – many of the research and teaching directions that I developed and guided them into. I can remember when they were neophytes, and now I see

Andrew D. Cohen

them taking on many of the roles that I had assumed in my own career. I know they are very appreciative of everything that I did for them and they are quick to acknowledge my contributions, both to me and to others. This, then, is a very special joy of being a professor.

Having students teach me about developments in a field, for example by referring me to readings that I was unaware of – including articles that they themselves have written, providing me new ideas and new ways of thinking about an academic issue.

When I started the process of teaching and mentoring my students, in some ways I was on a pedestal and students were looking up to me. As time went by, however, some of my better students shifted their roles in relationship to me. They got so accomplished in one or another field I had taught them that they were now able to provide me with insights from the field about which I was unaware. For example, they did extensive reading in one or more fields that gave them new ideas about certain issues with which I had been grappling. So, with respect to these issues, they became or have become my teacher. Given my openness to this kind of role shift, it was and continues to be an enormous joy.

Creating entirely new courses and new programs that are well received by the students.

In some ways developing new courses, especially as part of a new program, can be very challenging. Professors may not be sure just how students are going to respond both to a new program and to the new courses that are being offered. So, it was all the more gratifying when I found that my students were truly pleased with the courses and happy to be in the program. Perhaps the ultimate compliment was to learn after I retired from teaching at the University of Minnesota that a course I had created, "Practical Language Learning for International Communication," had become a multi-section offering every semester. It gave me great joy to witness this development in that I had created the course out of a sense that there was a gap which such a course could fill. Its successful continuation and expansion serves in my mind as a validation of this effort at instructional innovation.

Walking out of a class session glowing with the satisfaction that the session went exactly as I had planned and that it clearly made a significant contribution to my students.

Sometimes I was not sure how well a given class session would go over. My intention was for it to contribute to my students, but there was usually an element of doubt in my mind. I often went out of my way to make sure that every class session contributed to my students in some meaningful way, but sometimes the magic just did not seem to be there for whatever reason. It may have been that the students I had in the course that year or semester were different from those I had had the last time I taught the class. It might be that I had misgivings about my own ability to put the material across (i.e., I was "off my game"). Perhaps I had been under the weather or had had family matters with which to deal. And possibly there were issues going on at my university campus or in society that were encroaching on what happened in my classroom. So, when a class session worked just as I had planned, making it the kind of contribution that I was aiming for, then in my mind it was as if fireworks had gone off when I left the class. The satisfaction that I experienced was usually a huge source of joy.

Getting everything in the lesson plan accomplished in the allotted time without rushing things.

Professors often create lesson plans for a class session and then run out of time before accomplishing all that they had planned. After all, it can be a daunting task to "guesstimate" just how much time is needed to cover the intended material in a class session, allowing for individual, group, and paired interactions, as well as for class discussion – especially when there is limited time. Hence, it was gratifying to find that when a class period was over, I had, in fact, covered all that I had intended to cover, even without rushing through the material. When this happened, it was likely to make me feel better about myself as a professor, in that at least with regard to lesson planning, I seemed to have my act together.

Having the extra time and effort I had put into the preparation and delivery of a course reflected in the generally positive ratings that my course was given by my students.

Students can be stern critics of their professors' professorial act. The reasons for this are understandable. Tertiary-level education has gotten more expensive, which makes it more of a challenge for students to be able to finance their studies. It may call for them to work long hours and therefore get less sleep in order to complete course assignments. Consequently, they may come to class tired, under financial stress, and therefore slightly on edge. This situation means that if they criticize their instructor, a bit of it may be prompted by their need to vent. Nonetheless, since students are likely to have differing learning style preferences, it is altogether probable that at least some students will criticize one or another aspect of a course, such as the presentations by the professor, the quality of the readings, or the nature of the course projects. The bottom line is that as much as a professor tries to cater to a panoply of students' needs, it is difficult to please all the students all of the time. In my case, for example, although some students were pleased with my anecdotes – intended to liven up class presentations and perhaps to help the students retain the lecture material – other students would indicate in the course evaluations that they saw these anecdotes as needless digressions. Hence, having students rate my courses positively was a true joy, especially in this age when students are providing critical reviews of restaurants in Yelp, of hotels in TripAdvisor, and of products in Amazon.

Andrew D. Cohen

Being asked to teach at an exclusive summer institute.

To be selected as one of the instructors for a prestigious summer institute is clearly a significant accomplishment in the career of a professor. The instructors chosen for these institutes are considered to be top experts in their respective fields. They are asked to teach in summer institutes because the organizers deem that their reputation in the field and their talents as an instructor will be a big draw in recruiting participants from all over the world. So, being invited to be one of these instructors is an acknowledgment of one's status as a professor in the field. How joyous it was for me then to be among the professors invited to teach one summer at the Summer Institute of Linguistics (at Cornell) and several times at the summer Applied Linguistics Institute (at Penn State University). It was also a joy to be able to interact with fine colleagues who were teaching in those institutes at the same time.

Contributing to the education of the next generation of scholars, who have taken over in the international arena just as I am winding down my career.

Especially as I stopped university teaching and phased into semi-retirement, I became mindful of the fact that in many arenas – especially that of classroom instruction – I was passing on the torch to the next generation of academics.

In some cases, they have reported to me that they are starting up where I had left off. On occasion, former students of mine have informed me that they still refer back to my class notes, that they use some of my course materials in their teaching, and that they draw on my instructional approaches in making their own contributions. This feedback is a joy for me to receive because it indicates that I had obviously been doing something right. In general, it has been a real source of joy to watch my own students become top experts in the field and to be admired by their students.

Andrew D. Cohen

PROFESSIONAL TALKS

Giving a special talk to a group, where I can see in the engagement of the listeners that I have initiated or enhanced their own thinking on the topic.

A challenge in giving academic talks – especially in the evening – is to keep the material engaging enough so that an audience will stay with the speaker through to the end. It helps to have a topic that the audience has not heard a talk about before. It helps if the speaker has created a clear niche by the way that the topic is addressed. The burden is still on the speaker to make sure that what the audience hears is fascinating. When giving a PowerPoint presentation, speakers may make an effort to ensure that the slides are riveting and are keeping the audience attentive. Ideally, listeners are hanging on every word and what the speaker is saying is so provocative that it motivates listeners to think deeply about the issues that are being raised. How rewarding it can be for me to have my words stimulate others to pursue the same theme on their own, whether to do some follow-up reading, to do some research on the topic, or to contact me after the talk to get my feedback on their thinking. Fortunately, in that I continue to give presentations at national and international meetings, I am still able to experience this kind of joy.

Giving a talk in a manner that produces numerous questions from the audience.

Some professors may feel that questions posed following a talk are an indication that issues were not adequately presented. However, it can also be the case that when a topic is presented clearly and perhaps provocatively, this may result in numerous hands going up – which launches into a fruitful discussion. When this happens, speakers should view it as a form of acknowledgement. If a major purpose for a talk is to stimulate thinking about a topic, then having a raft of questions and comments at the end can be a source of joy. I view the feedback that I receive from a talk as potentially helpful in going forward. Consequently, I do my best to take some notes during the Q and A and discussion expressly for this purpose. I view these questions as a source of joy, even if the questions themselves are ones that are difficult to answer and even if they are critical. In fact, the criticism can serve to help in revision of the paper that the presentation may be based on.

Having a group of participants come up to me after a talk to acknowledge my presentation and to ask me questions.

As I noted above, for me a measure of a successful talk is the number of questions posed at the end. In fact, an ideal situation is that there are so many questions that if there is a time constraint, I need to write the questions down and answer as many as time permits in some logical order. However, especially in some cultures, it may be considered rude to ask questions of the speaker at the end of a talk. It may be considered more appropriate to come up to the speaker after the talk to pose questions. It can be a joyous situation when a group of attendees at my talk gather around me to ask follow-up questions and to get my advice on the issues that I have raised.

Not having a clue as to what to say in a given talk and then having it all fall into place well – and perhaps even so well that the hosts want to invite me back to speak on the same or a different topic in the future.

Although it may be prestigious to be asked to give a talk, as the date of the talk approaches, I sometimes realize that what I have planned to speak on may not be as clear in my mind as what I had intended it to be when I agreed to give it. The issues of the talk usually ruminate in my mind for a few days before the talk and then just before the event itself, some keen insights may fortunately come to me – ones that really help me solidify my presentation in a significant way. If so, a talk that appeared to have reached an impasse is transformed into an opportunity for me to share my insights with an audience. The joy is both from these last-minute insights as well as from any confirmation I received afterwards regarding my presentation. One tangible example of feedback is when after my talk my hosts indicate to me that they would like to invite me back in the future for a follow-up talk. This has happened to me in Singapore, Japan, South Korea, China, Greece, and after talks in other cities as well.

Surprising myself at my ability to work my way through nervousness, stage fright, or even panic that I don't have much of value to say.

There are times in my career when I have found myself speaking in front of a large crowd – say, over 800 people. Facing large groups can be disconcerting for professors, especially if they have imagined that the audience's sole purpose was to find fault with what they were saying, how they were saying it, or both. Over the years, I have found a way to turn this potentially confrontational encounter into a joy. It is to focus on what I have to contribute to

Andrew D. Cohen

my audience. Assuming I do have something special to offer them, keeping focused as much as possible on that, and not on the fact that so many people are listening to me, has helped me get over stage fright. By focusing just on what it is I have to offer, I find it does not matter so much how many people are in the audience. In fact, I may assume the attitude that "the more the merrier." In this way I am able to convert what could otherwise be a potential nightmare into a joy.

Finding that I really do have something significant to say and that I am able to say it in an intelligible way.

Sometimes when I am planning a talk, I may not be sure that I have something insightful to offer. For this reason, I may be somewhat reticent to even present it, out of fear that people listening to me may see through my arguments and may consider my presentation unhelpful at best. So how pleasant it can be when I learn that what I presented resonated with listeners, and perhaps put into words what they had been thinking about but had not stated in that fashion. In these instances, my colleagues let me know just how much they appreciated what I said, either in person just after my talk or perhaps through a follow-up email. This kind of feedback can help to allay my misgivings and replace them with a sense of joy that the talk was worth giving and possibly even transformational for the listeners.

Finding that a talk I worked so hard on for another meeting is just perfect for the current one as well, so I need not worry about hours more of preparation.

Preparing a talk, especially a plenary or keynote address, may take a long time, especially if it calls for thinking outside the box and for checking sources very carefully. In addition, hours may be devoted to preparing PowerPoint slides. So, imagine how pleasing it can be to discover that some talk already given is totally appropriate for another venue as well – for an audience that would not have heard the previous talk. For me, the joy is especially real if I had planned on preparing a new talk before I had the insight that a previous one fills the bill for the new venue as well, even if it involves tweaking the talk to make it more relevant to the current venue. Then I find myself with extra time on my hands – to spend time with my family, go to the beach, read a new book for my men's book club, smell the roses, or whatever.

Viewing a videotape of a talk I have given and being surprised that my performance came out better than I had thought.

It is generally unsettling to view a video-recording of a talk one has given. Especially striking when viewing the video may be some mannerisms that one was totally unaware of – such as excessive use of hands and arms, looking down at notes too much, too many filled pauses (uh's and uhm's), and an overabundance of digressions. Imagine, then, my surprise when I have watched portions of a recently recorded video talk and found that I have actually performed well – without an abundance of distracting mannerisms and consistent with the audience reactions that I received. It can be a real joy to have the actual performance exceed expectations.

Coaching graduate students in the successful presentation of conference papers and then having them report back afterwards that their presentations went well.

Especially these days, it can be a real achievement to have a proposal accepted for presentation at a conference – especially in one of the major associations where the conference organizers may accept only a small percentage of the submissions for presentation. One half of the battle is having a proposal accepted. The other half is giving a memorable presentation. This was a real concern to me when I was a relative newcomer to the field and anxious to establish myself.

During my University of Minnesota years, I came up with an entertaining way of coaching graduate students to prepare effective conference presentations. What I did was to give as poor a presentation as I possibly could to a group of graduate students. In other words, I stayed seated behind a table during my presentation, I read from a cryptic text rarely looking up to make eye contact with the audience, I mumbled and did so relatively quickly so that it was difficult to understand what I was saying, and then I made sure to use up all my allotted time so that there was no time for questions. In other words, I did my best to deviate from many of the rules about how to present effectively. After this lackluster performance, I divided the graduate students into two groups. One group was given the mandate to discuss among themselves what I did wrong. The other group was given the task of discussing strategies for delivering an outstanding presentation. The two groups then reported back to all the participants with their findings and suggestions.

In a follow-up session I invited graduate students – especially those with upcoming presentations – to give practice presentations. Rather than having them do the entire talk, they were instead invited to give just their introduction, excerpts from the body of the talk, and then the conclusions. Supportive critique was then afforded them by fellow graduate students and by me. It was a tremendous joy to hear back from graduate students after they had given their conference presentations, that their session went well, possibly even garnering accolades from listeners. One never knows at the time just how impactful a given talk can be for a career.

The feeling of accomplishment I have experienced when I am invited to give a plenary or keynote talk at an upcoming meeting, perhaps several years away.

There are just so many slots for plenary or keynote addresses

Andrew D. Cohen

at any given meeting. Often, it seems as if the same colleagues are always being invited to give presentations, usually because of their status in the field through their publications, presentations, and depth of knowledge. Hence, it may be all the more satisfying for me to be invited to give a plenary or keynote address. Of course, along with the elation at being recognized as an academic with something special to provide the conference goers, there is also the realization that I will need to devote much time and energy to living up to the expectations of the conference organizers. Nonetheless, this in no way detracts from the obvious joy associated with receiving the invitation, especially when it was the first time I was invited to give a plenary address at a meeting.

Being selected as a plenary speaker at a meeting where the other speakers are all renowned scholars in their respective areas of specialization.

Just as it can be special to be asked to be a plenary or keynote speaker at a conference, it is even more of a joy to learn that the other scholars invited to speak are all highly respected. This fact can enhance the joy many times over. It can also be a joy for me to have some quality visit time with one or more of them, especially when we have not yet had a chance for a personal visit. In fact, when looking back at my career over the years, some of my highest quality moments at conferences have been thanks to the opportunity to have individual interactions with leading scholars in the field, which would not have been the case had I not had these special invitations to speak.

Giving a talk that provides an honorarium

Although not so common anymore, it used to be a joy to be offered an honorarium, however modest – a financial stipend beyond airfare and hotel expenses to give a talk. Although an honorarium used to be an expected part of an invitation to speak at an academic conference, these days the invitation is usually limited to reimbursement for airfare and hotel expenses. All the more gratifying then for me to be offered an honorarium for my participation. After all, I had to put in a good deal of time and effort preparing a talk and/or workshop, not to mention the effort of traveling to the venue and spending time there.

TRIPS AND TRAVELING

Taking funded trips to special places that I really wanted to visit, thanks to a conference, a course I was teaching, or some other academic event.

While it is not a given that choosing a professorial career will entail funded travel to attractive spots around the globe, it may very well be the case, especially if an area of expertise has international currency. Nowadays, given the globalization of so many academic disciplines (such as mine in applied linguistics/second language studies), conferences in academic domains are increasingly taking place in exotic locations around the world, such as in Famagusta, Turkish Cyprus. As for courses, while they may involve travel, more are being conducted through Skype or other social media venues on the Internet. In addition, some research projects have also sent me repeatedly to a far away world venue, such as trips to Doha in Qatar.

When I have had the opportunity take these kinds of trips, they have added great joy to my life. It is like getting two for the price of one: I have gotten the academic stimulation from the event, plus the added joy of getting to know other parts of the world better, without having to spend a lot of money on a vacation there. Whereas a business trip is often characterized as a quick in and out, an academic trip usually affords me (and if possible, my spouse) some quality visit time while at these sites. It has also given me the opportunity to spend a day with a valued colleague doing some local sightseeing, perhaps with a guide. These forays have been ones that I often think back on with joy.

Not only being invited to fascinating places in the world for academic reasons, but finding some of my special collegial friends have also been invited, enabling us to enjoy the venue together.

Sometimes when I am fantasizing, I see myself living on an imaginary street where my neighbors are, in fact, also my colleagues who are also dear friends, hence "colleague-friends." In this fantasy realm, I have a chance to interact with them on a regular basis. The reality is that some of my dearest colleague-friends and I are likely to have a chance for quality visits with each other only every several years. Even if there is some annual conference in our field that we attend, we may end up having only brief encounters because these events can be a bit hectic. All the more reason why it can be a super joy to have time to spend with these special colleague-friends when we are invited to present at a meeting, engage in a research project together, or co-teach a course. It may be at these venues where I really have invaluable opportunities to share about important, sometimes life-sustaining matters. In principle, an email, a phone call, or a text message could all serve the purpose of linking me with a special friend in a field, but for many busy academics, this kind of quality time is unlikely to happen without some special occasion such as those enumerated above.

Having international colleagues who host me (as well as my family members when possible) in their cities and in their homes all over the world.

In a career as a professor, while I may not have had a high salary as compared to those in other professions, the position has afforded me a level of prestige which at times can be most gratifying. Especially in certain countries, professors tend to be held in particularly high esteem. Given this preferential status, sometimes when I travel to other states within the USA and often when it is to other countries, I find the level of hosting by colleagues most impressive – especially when it is by those who are my former students or colleagues that I have mentored in meaningful ways. Suffice it to say that paying them a visit in their respective home venues may result in far more special attention than may have been expected. What a joy this can be, especially in communities where knowing someone in a special way makes my stay truly memorable. In Japan, it has meant being invited to a colleague's home, which is something that rarely happens on an ordinary basis. In Brazil, it has meant being invited to a colleague's *sitio*, which is a complex of buildings out in the country, often including a residence, a swimming pool, a ping-pong room, servants' quarters, and so forth.

Not only having all my travel expenses to some far away and exotic place paid for by others, but also having a great time both academically and socially once I am there.

It may be that the reputation and publications of professors result in their receiving an invitation to attend a meeting in some relatively remote corner of the world. One example of this is the invitation that I received to give a plenary at a meeting in Famagusta, Turkish Cyprus. The invitation served as an opportunity for me not only to travel to this venue, but also to learn about the politics of the region. Had I not received this invitation, it is unlikely that I would ever have gone to such a relatively remote place. Now that I have been there, I feel more knowledgeable about that specific part of the world and have a better understanding of the local people and their various cultures. The joy is in having my career as a professor be a vehicle for adding new venues to my knowledge of the world and to my understanding of peoples.

Andrew D. Cohen

Arriving at some professional event in a far-off part of the world new to me and finding that colleagues not only want me to autograph a copy of a book of mine, but also would like their picture taken with me.

Professors who publish extensively may find that, unbeknownst to them, many people throughout the world are reading their works. Especially in this new global reality where peoples of the world are brought closer together through the Internet, and with the addition of e-books, the likelihood is that more people than ever before in the academic community are accessing publications and having positive reactions to them. Consequently, when I arrive at a conference in a country where I do not have a coterie of known colleagues (such as in Manila, the Philippines), I may be treated by conference goers as if I am a celebrity. For example, they may line up to request my autograph in a copy of my latest book or ask to have a picture taken with me. I had thought that this behavior was reserved for writers of popular fiction rather than for writers of scholarly works. Yet to my surprise, I have an found that it has applied to me as well, which has been a true joy at the time.

Being able to visit and give professional talks in parts of the world where colleagues could not fund my trip, thanks to a paid trip to some other nearby site.

Serendipity can play a role in a professor's career, with the result being that of pure joy. I have been invited to give professional talks in a part of the world where colleagues do not have the funds to cover my travel expenses. Whereas I may wish to make the trip because of my commitment to the field or interest in the topic, as retiree I may be reluctant to pay for my own ticketing. Then, out of the blue, I get invited by colleagues from a country relatively near the one from which I had received the unfunded invitation. This new invitation enables me to just "hop over to" the neighboring country either before or after visiting the one that is paying my way. It is almost as if the colleagues with the funding somehow knew of my desire to accommodate the wishes of those lacking the financial support. I see this as part of the melody of life, wherein things happen that cannot be explained rationally. Rather, it is perhaps a form of divine providence at work. One time that this happened to me, whereas my financially-strapped hosts did not have money for my air ticket, they actually were able to provide me sumptuous local accommodations, including delicious meals and delightful entertainment, all the while that I was making an academic contribution to their students and faculty, as well as to others in their academic community.

RESEARCH AND SCHOLARSHIP

Having the freedom to select the topics on which I will do research and how I will do it.

One of the great pleasures for me in being an academic in the USA is that in the institutions in which I taught (UCLA, the Hebrew University of Jerusalem, and the University of Minnesota), I experienced total freedom with regard to the topics that I did research on and the research methods that I used. Obviously, there were limits to this freedom, especially when my funding source(s) set certain guidelines as to the nature of the research in a particular area. In some instances, it entailed bringing in experts in that area to support my research effort. But often the topic that I selected for any given study was largely or exclusively of my choosing. In fact, noteworthy academic research is often characterized by finding a unique topic or niche, one that is more likely to be of interest to colleagues when published.

There is, in fact, usually so much freedom that the myriad of required research decisions (e.g., about how many participants to recruit for a sample and who the participants will be, whether or not the study will have mixed methods, what instruments will be used, and what statistics will be employed to analyze the results) are often left entirely in the professors' hands. At times, the full realization of the extent of one's research freedom can be frightening. On the other hand, there can and should be enormous joy associated with the research effort, in the sense that professors are engaged in a form of creation and will most likely have full license to craft the research as they choose. This has certainly been my experience in designing research projects.

Designing a research project to be carried out in the local schools and finding school administrators, teachers, and pupils are really happy to have me do it there.

One of the potential hurdles associated with doing a research project is finding research participants who are amenable to participating, given that the study may call for some hours of participation on their part. Often, the more rigorous the study is – involving a series of measures, one more engaging than the next – the more likely it is that the participants may come to feel a bit victimized. They may even have a sense that they are being slightly exploited. Obstacles can also be laid in the path of the most well-intentioned study involving elementary-level, middle-school, or high-school pupils by their parents, who may well claim that they are not paying for their children's education for them to be participants in a research study. Hence, it may be crucial to win over the support of this group as well. Usually institutional review boards provide guidance to academics to ensure cooperation from parents when K-12 students are involved.

Given the potential threats to the successful completion of a study, it has been a truly joyous moment for me when I have received feedback from the administrators at a given school, from the teachers, and also from the participating students that a completed study was one in which the various parties involved were positive about the study, and that the participants in the study found that the measures served as an eye-opener to them about the issues involved. After all, beneficial research – such as in an applied field – is intended to have a positive impact, in this case with regard to language instruction. One would hope and expect that the research effort would have the participants taking a closer look at some aspect of what pedagogical practices actually entail. A real tribute to the study is when the participants request a copy of the written report because they are so eager to learn from it.

Finding that some of the participants in the data collection phase of my research study are special people and that it has been a treat to get to know them.

Professors usually do not know until they start collecting their data just who the participants are. Depending on the nature of the study, it may be imperative to keep a distance from the subjects and not influence the nature of the data that they provide. This may not be the case when using, for example, verbal report as a means for obtaining think-aloud, introspective, and retrospective data, which entails tapping the minds of the participants while they are performing one or another task. In this case there may be a need to provide them orientation as to how they are expected to respond, in order that the data are focused on the issues of concern in the study.

Especially in cases where I have had more extensive contact with my participants, it can be especially joyous to learn that one or another of them are fascinating people and that it is my distinct honor to have them in my sample. This in itself can be a joy since often in research, participants are kept at a distance and even objectified in some ways. But when I collect and analyze the data, I have been able to see that some of the participants are special individuals. They have a sense of my research goals and have furnished me crystal clear data that go a long way to providing the kinds of insights that I have wanted in my study.

Devising a new means for collecting empirical data or enhancing an existing one so much that others now find it beneficial to use it in their own research thanks to my efforts.

To become a professor, I had to pass through a series of roles, perhaps the most memorable being that of a graduate student. During that stage, I took various courses at Stanford University on research methods, which included learning about research techniques that people were using in the field. Then there came a point in my professorial career where I was not only using some of these techniques, but also innovating. Whereas I did not devise totally new ways to collect data, I was involved in significantly enhancing at least one technique that existed but that was not being used as it could have been – namely, verbal report. As a tribute to my work, I was asked to write an entry about it in an encyclopedic volume on applied linguistics. The fact is that I went from a consumer to a respected contributor when it came to certain research methods. This was a source of joy to me in my career. In other words, not only have I received acknowledgement for the results of my research, but also for the means that were used to obtain those results.

Having the results of a research study come out in the expected way.

When conducting research, there is usually a question as to what the results will be. Even after careful piloting of measures with participants similar to those in the main study, one can never be sure that the results will come out the way that was predicted. While it can be an exciting feature of research to have totally unexpected results, it can still be immensely reassuring to find that the results are consistent with original predictions, and perhaps more so than expected. Especially in studies where my participants have provided me with data richer than I had anticipated, I have viewed those results as a confirmation that the efforts I expended in the data collection procedures were worthwhile. The joy associated with this realization has been a cause for celebration.

Getting totally unexpected research results that are nonetheless interpretable and that lead to a whole series of new investigations.

I have also experienced joy when the findings of a study are not consistent with my expectations. This too can be a valuable and actually enjoyable part of the research process. Open and unbiased exploration allows for results that while not predicted can nonetheless open the door to new explorations aimed at finding out why the predictions were off base. So, just when I was wondering what I could possibly do next if the results had been consistent with what I predicted, I now have some new research ventures in which to engage.

Making a discovery in a research context and having it successfully applied in real-world contexts afterwards.

For professors in an applied field, it can be pleasing to do research and have the findings be so useful that they are successfully applied in a real-world context, such as language pedagogy. Obviously, this is not a given. It depends greatly on just how well the research is designed and conducted to make sure the findings are convincing. The point is that applied research has an ultimate goal of producing findings that in one way or another have applications to the real world. What a joy it has been for me to see this happen in different contexts – fifth- and sixth-graders enhancing their strategies for both learning and performing in a Spanish full-immersion classroom, college students getting a better handle on the learning and use of language in their college courses and beyond, and graduate students obtaining a better understanding regarding the functions of strategies when they endeavor to fine-tune their comprehension of academic vocabulary in a second or foreign language.

Andrew D. Cohen

Arriving at categorizing successfully a set of items appearing in the research literature, then constructing a scheme of classification for these items, and finally validating this classification scheme empirically.

Just as I enjoy tidying up a closet or drawer that seems in need of order, I have found that I like to categorize items that are presented in an apparently disparate fashion in the research literature. Over the years, I have even had an epiphany or two regarding a possible scheme of classification that would make order out of relative disorder. Consequently, I have conducted research and have encouraged others to do research that helps to validate a classification scheme. The result is a new classification of items in a given domain of research that becomes widely accepted in the field. This effort in classification has brought me joy in that it has contributed to the rigor of my academic thinking, as well as to that of others around the world.

Reading an M.A. thesis or a Ph.D. dissertation that is so fascinating for the ideas that it contains and the new ground that it covers that I feel privileged to have had the opportunity.

The fact is that the emergence of an M.A. thesis or a Ph.D. dissertation is a rather local event. Unless one knows about a particular student – perhaps by virtue of being at the same institution or coming across a citation of the student's work

– it is unlikely to come across the work unless or until it is published in the field, or at least until it is cited in some published work. There are simply too many such works being generated around the world all the time for me to be fully up on this literature. Hence, it can be almost accidental for me to become aware of these sometimes excellent contributions. It is, of course, possible to search through dissertation databases and to pay what it is now an exorbitant fee to get a copy of a dissertation. When I was a visiting faculty member at Auckland University in New Zealand, I discovered that their library provided free access to any doctoral dissertation that was referenced in the database of any university worldwide. Needless to say, I downloaded many dissertations – perhaps 35. Most universities allow free access to a limited number of dissertations. For example the University of Minnesota only gave access to dissertations from Big-Ten Universities in the Midwest. The challenge is to find the ones that benefit me in my work, and when I do, it can be a source of sheer delight. Fortunately, more students are now posting their theses and dissertations on academic websites, or on their own website.

Feeling that I have presented my side convincingly in a highly contested argument in the literature and then having colleagues tell me so.

It can be a lonely process to make a case with regard to a contentious issue in a given field. In fact, at times I sometimes feel as if I am the only one who clearly sees that "the Emperor has no clothing" – in other words, that the case that other colleagues are making is specious. So when I do make my case, I may really feel as if I am going out on a very long limb without a safety net. So, imagine my joy when after my views have been published, others in the field speak out and agree with me. In some cases, they may have been reluctant to voice support for this side of an argument publicly for fear that a rebuke might cost them status in the field. As it turns out, the fact that I articulated my side of the argument so forcefully has given them space to come out in support of this side of the argument. The point is that sometimes in academia, joy may be derived from "screwing my courage to the sticking place" and taking a stand for others to join me in my stand.

Establishing a presence in the research literature so that my name and accomplishments are known and valued in my area(s) of expertise in the field.

While giving conference presentations and teaching short courses regionally has helped make me known in the field, publishing widely is often the main vehicle for this to happen, and especially when I have published articles in journals with high readership, along with chapters in seminal volumes, such as handbooks and other valued collections of papers. It has also helped to write books that are published internationally and are re-published by local presses in China and elsewhere. I also have one co-authored book that has been translated from English into both Japanese and Arabic, and is currently being translated into Korean. In the case of this translation of a book on the teaching and learning of pragmatics into Korean, I must admit that some years ago I gave a plenary to an international association of Korean language teachers on this theme, and that this talk may have planted the seed that resulted some years later in having the book translated into Korean. I can say that having my work at this level of visibility in the academic world is a source of joy.

Needless to say, heightened visibility also means more work for me. For example, I receive a steady stream of requests to review submissions to journals where I feel obligated to review them because they cite my work. In addition, I receive proposals to evaluate new books in fields with which I am associated. Likewise, I am asked to review candidates for new positions or for promotion to more senior academic positions at their institutions. My visibility in the field has also meant being asked to write a book in some series where I had not considered such a project.

WRITING AND EDITING

Being asked by a respected publisher in my field to write a book in an area of my expertise.

Over the course of my career the thought of writing a new book has always produced mixed emotions, because I know how much work it entails, usually over several years. When it is an empirically-based book, I know that it will involve both a rigorous reading of the research literature, and most likely the conducting of an empirical study calling for the development of instruments as well as a thorough analysis of the data. In addition, I am aware that given the current climate around publications, publishers may be reluctant to engage authors in new writing projects unless they are confident that the author is likely to be successful with the project and that the finished book will attract sales.

All the more joy, then, to be contacted by a leading publisher in my field and to be asked whether I would like to write a new book for their company in one of my areas of expertise. In the case of my most recent book on pragmatics, the editors of a popular book series by a leading publishing house in applied linguistics attended a keynote address that I gave at a meeting and came up to me at the end of my presentation to personally ask me to develop the material into a book. The advantage here is that I knew that the book would have a venue for publication once I had finished writing it. In addition, it is highly flattering to have representatives from such a prominent publishing house being so interested in my work and confident in my abilities. The book came out at the end of May, 2018. It was a joy to see it emerge.

Editing or co-editing a volume where it all comes together magically

Professors who have edited or co-edited a book are aware that it can be a most arduous undertaking. Perhaps they have been in the role of co-editor for a collection of conference papers in need of being collected up, edited, and published. The scenario for such efforts often involves the editors having to pursue the chapter authors for some months or years until they produce the write-up of their conference presentation. Whereas they may have been requested to come to the meeting with finished papers, this is often not the case. Hence, these presenters need to write their papers, which may take some time. This means that those contributors who efficiently submitted their chapters well before or at the time of the deadline may find themselves waiting around for months until the volume is actually ready to be submitted for publication. This poses a bit of a juggling match for the editors since they need to remember which submissions they edited when, to avoid duplication of efforts. Then the editors need to write a convincing, appealing introduction to the volume, as well as a solid conclusion, tying together all the various themes that are presented in the book. This can be a daunting task when the conference had a series of sometimes disparate themes woven together.

Among the four co-editing experiences that I have

had in my career, a highly joyous one was a volume on language learner strategy research with Ernesto Macaro for Oxford University Press. It was truly amazing when all those selected to submit their papers as chapters in the edited volume did so with efficiency and alacrity, such that the volume was ready for publication in record time. The contributors' responses to our editorial comments were prompt and contributory. Adding to the amazement, when my co-editor and I agreed to write our own separate conclusion for the volume, we found that our two renditions of the conclusion actually complemented each other so well that they could be interwoven as one conclusion in a seamless fashion. This, then, contributed to the magic of a well-edited volume.

In all fairness, what can help to ensure a successfully edited volume is that the book not be of disparate conference presentations, but rather of papers derived from a well-organized meeting of colleagues, such as the book on language learner strategy research which I co-edited. At the meeting that produced this volume, there were no formal presentations as such, but rather a series of working sessions – where colleagues committed themselves to specific working groups before the meeting started. The papers, then, were a follow-up to those working sessions, such that the authors were committed to doing the work in a timely fashion. So, while it was a joy to see the edited volume come to fruition, it was from the beginning a highly orchestrated effort. That, too, can be a significant part of what makes the completion of a volume truly joyous.

Grappling with a piece of writing and then having a breakthrough where it all comes together nicely.

Even well-published professors may at times feel stymied – where they do not really have a sense as to how to proceed with a given article or chapter. They may have done a fine job of outlining their writing, but then find when they get to a certain sub-topic, they really do not know what to write. The joy is to get insights leading to a significant breakthrough and then subsequently complete the writing task. The insights may come from referring to one or more readings in the field. They may come from interactions with colleagues or they may be the result of looking back at some previous publication and having the way it was written assist in the current writing project. It is also possible that these insights seem to come out of the blue, since being stuck gives the mind a chance to ruminate about issues. So, perhaps it is the very breakdown in the writing that leads to the breakthrough. In any event, the completion of a writing assignment has seemed all the sweeter for me if I have successfully overcome whatever obstacle it was that was blocking my path.

Getting such helpful feedback from colleagues about a piece I am writing that I now see what I did not see before about how to improve it.

When I am in the midst of writing a paper, I may feel reluctant to share the draft with colleagues because of its incomplete nature – feeling that this would expose me to criticism. How palpable my joy is when I do share a draft with colleagues and find that their input really helps to improve the paper, giving me direction for how to finish it in a productive way. My colleagues may, for example, suggest citing certain sources that I had not thought of or known about. By citing them, I find that I have better situated my piece in the academic literature. Of course, it is also possible to get highly constructive and useful feedback from anonymous reviewers when submitting a paper for possible publication in a journal. It can be a real joy to have a reviewer give feedback that clearly serves to enhance the quality of the paper.

Working together with a colleague to compose a joint paper, and being able to benefit from two heads thinking of what to write rather than just one.

Over the course of my career, there have been times when writing a paper with one or more colleagues who focus on their areas of expertise while I focus on mine – constituting a partnering of the best kind – has been joyous. Likewise, it has been a joy to write ostensibly on the same topic as a colleague and to find that our writings complement each other nicely because of our differing perspectives on what we are writing about, allowing us to then combine them. In the writing up of a research study, it can be a joy when the team members take responsibility for writing up the part of the study in which they were involved.

Having an article accepted for publication.

If I am writing a chapter or a book, I almost always have secured a venue for publication in advance. The chapters that I write are usually solicited by editors, and with regard to books, the series editors for a publishing house have usually invited me to write it, and I then have a signed contract with them. In itself this is a joy. With an article, however, it is often the case that I am looking for a journal in which to publish it. In such instances, I am beholden to anonymous reviewers who act as gatekeepers for the given journal. Especially if it is a tier-1 journal, it may be a real challenge to get an article accepted for publication. The reviewers may simply not see the merits of a particular contribution. Suffice it to say that lots of new journals have sprung up – especially free online ones – in response to the fact that the established journals these days are rejecting many more submissions then they used to. And if an article of mine is accepted for publication, a likely scenario is that substantive revisions are requested. Needless to say, the joy is in managing to jump through all the hoops and in seeing my publication emerge.

I should also point out that it has been a joy for me in my career not just to be published in tier-1 journals such as the *Modern Language Journal*, but also in lesser-known journals or even extremely local ones, in order to bring my work to readers of those publications, as well as to perhaps bolster the status of the publications.

Having a manuscript accepted for publication in a refereed journal or rigorously edited book without having to do many revisions.

As suggested above, it is somewhat anomalous these days to have a journal article or book chapter accepted without having to do extensive revision. For one thing, since publishing is increasingly expensive, it is often the case that the author is asked to shorten the manuscript, sometimes by as much as 25%. This may call for crafty wordsmithing, as well as cutting out what could be perceived as an essential part of the manuscript. For another thing, as the academic literature expands, it is increasingly likely that the reviewers will request a modification of the review of literature to include authors or topics which had been left out, either out of ignorance or because an author did not think something was relevant. If a manuscript is to be published, the author usually needs to respond in a detailed fashion to the reviewers' comments. In other words, an author may be expected to respond to each comment or query provided by a reviewer, either by rebutting the point and giving a justification, or by accepting it and indicating what was done in the paper to accommodate it. Regardless of the selected approach, the process is time-consuming and sometimes fraught with obstacles. Consequently, it has been all the more joyous for me when a journal informs me that my article has (finally) been accepted for publication.

Finishing up some major or minor publication and being able to send it off electronically.

This is more likely to be a joy for those who are more compulsive about finishing things. For those who really enjoy arriving at the point where a paper or book is ready to be sent off for editors and reviewers to respond to, the moment of completion can be highly significant and joyous. Needless to say, because the trajectory from this point to the emergence of the publication itself may be long and sometimes arduous, the initiation of this process by attaching my document and pushing the "send" key can trigger some level of euphoria on my part.

I can remember the days before electronic submissions when I used to have to photocopy and mail multiple hardcopy versions of my writing and perhaps worry about whether or not the package would get to the editors in a timely fashion. This dramatic change in the submission process can itself spark joy – the very fact that submissions can be enacted instantly. Moreover, if I am submitting to an automated system, which is the norm now for journal submissions, I also get immediate feedback as to whether my submission is, on the face of things, acceptable (e.g., with an abstract of appropriate length, a text within the word limit, and numerous other tidbits of information).

Seeing an article, a chapter, or a book appear in print.

At the end of the trajectory – sometimes months later, when the writing appears as a publication, there is the joy of seeing it out in the field. If this publication is in a tier-1 journal or in a seminal volume on some topic, it may be an especially joyous occasion to see it emerge. Thinking back to my earliest publications, I was thrilled to see any publication emerge. In truth, it is still a source of pleasure to see my publications emerge in that it constitutes a form of completion in knowing that this particular goal is now achieved and that I can move on to others. In fact, this is still true in my semi-retirement, when I no longer "need" to publish in order to improve my status at a given university.

Receiving a copy of a book that I wrote, edited, or contributed to – all nicely printed and packaged.

Having the publication in hand is gratifying in that it is a joy to see my words nicely printed in a volume. This makes what I have written somehow more respectable, more official, given that I still remember the days when my earlier drafts were handwritten and messy. Nowadays, it is also more common for publications to be disseminated and read electronically. While there are those who still prefer to read a printed version of a book, there are now many people – especially of the Kindle and Nook generation – who have become accustomed to accessing text digitally. One advantage of publishing digitally is that dissemination can be instantaneous worldwide. This is a huge advantage for scholars and students located in remote parts of the world where mail delivery can be spotty at best. It means that access to my writings has been elevated to a remarkable new level. This in itself can be an enormous source of joy.

Having a respected colleague write a highly positive review of a book that I wrote.

Once a book is out, then then it is open to review, which could mean anything from rants to raves. As an author I need to have a rather tough skin in order not to take any criticism I may receive too much to heart. It gives me solace to know that my publications have gone through a rigorous vetting process and would not have been published had they not passed muster. Publishers are clever these days including back-cover quotes from luminaries in the field highlighting what they consider to be outstanding features of the book. This approach may steal some of the thunder from potential critics. In addition, it would be inappropriate for these luminaries to then write a negative review of the book.

It may be that if there are negative reviews, they come from colleagues with their own agenda – which may include protecting what they consider to be their turf. In a best-case scenario, the praise far outweighs the criticism, and includes compliments on aspects that I simply took for granted. Suffice it to say that a positive review is a joy for me to read. Such a review may well serve as an affirmation of what I intended to do, and so provides an acknowledgment of my efforts. Positive reviews are also likely to promote sales, which can be yet another source of joy.

Having one or more seminal pieces selected for reprinting in an anthology of major works in the field.

While it is certainly satisfying for professors to be acknowledged for journal articles or book chapters at the time of publication, it can also be a joy to have the work recognized some years later as significant enough to be identified as worthy of reprinting in an anthology of what are considered seminal works on a given topic. This then gives a publication new life, especially since there will be readers who did not see it in its original venue, but now get to enjoy it in this new collection which is intended to showcase significant works in the field.

Serving as reviewer of a journal submission and having a significant role in its transformation from unpublishable to published.

The role of a reviewer of journal articles is largely an unsung one in that one is likely to spend hours meticulously reviewing papers with the only recompense being that if they ultimately appear, it may have been the reviewer's constructive comments – as well as those of others – that led the authors to producing a well-received article.

Professors may even be reluctant to take on the commitment of reviewing a given submission – especially the write-up of a research study – because they can see at the front end just how much work it will take. For example, they may need to spell out ways in which the submitted version is out of touch with the current research literature, is lacking in detail with regard to the research methodology, has not framed the research questions in an effective way, or has framed them acceptably but does not adequately answer them in the Findings section. Furthermore, the write-up of the study may deviate from an acceptable format for such articles in that inadequate attention is given to matters such as the study's limitations, suggestions for future research, and pedagogical implications. If a study has serious flaws in its conception and execution, it actually can make the reviewer's job easier. When a study is well conceived and executed but written up in an ineffectual manner, it can be the reviewer's role to provide the necessary guidance to make the study publishable – assuming that the reviewer has the patience to take on this role.

Andrew D. Cohen

While it can be a super joy to receive a submission that is so outstanding that the task of the reviewer is simply to acknowledge its excellence, it is more likely the case that once I agree to review something, it will take me a considerable amount of time to do a good job. It is especially in cases like these that after perhaps several revisions based on my extensive input and that of several other reviewers, I have the joy of watching the study emerge in print.

Generating publications with the awareness that some of them may help to shape the thinking of others.

At the start of my professorial career I certainly did not have aspirations to become widely published. In fact, at that time, just seeing one or two publications emerge was enough to give me joy. As I became more senior in the field, I was aware that a number of the publications that I generated were having a global impact.

In the early phase of my career I had to count the number of my publications since my university at the time evaluated my professorial standing in the field on the basis of numbers of publications (even numbers of pages), the prestige level of the given journal, and so forth. Especially as I gained seniority in the field, it was no longer a matter of number of publications, but rather of their impact. I have derived satisfaction from the feedback received in messages from students and colleagues, and from my "fans" at conferences.

Getting positive feedback from both students and colleagues for command of academic prose.

As a writer who is fortunately able to convey ideas in an accessible way, students and colleagues have on occasion acknowledged me for my ability with words – which I take for granted. Students often report finding themselves having to read texts that are not written in so accessible a fashion. It is gratifying when colleagues seek out my writings since they know that I make an effort to be intelligible, even when the topic can be a bit turgid (e.g. language assessment). One reason that my writings are readable is that I take an inordinate amount of time to make sure that this is the case, usually through doing multiple drafts. All the more so than is my joy when students and colleagues point out to me that my writings are readable. I credit much of my articulateness to my mother who would always be a great sparring partner, and who would encourage me to make my case clearly and effectively.

Helping to set up a new journal, guiding it through the initial phases to a point where it becomes an established and respected entity in the field.

In my career, I have found myself in the role of participant or advisor in the construction of a new journal. My participation has consisted of helping my colleagues to think through just what this new journal will entail in terms of topics to be covered, procedures for soliciting submissions, standards for accepting papers, and a host of other issues. I have also served on editorial boards for journals, and from time to time have been able to provide my colleagues with ideas from my experience on how to make this new journal venture work and work well. Seeing this journal take on a presence in the field has provided me satisfaction. My joy is derived from knowing that my input had an impact on the outcome, especially when this journal clearly provides a venue for the writings of many colleagues whose submissions are especially appropriate for a journal of this nature.

PROGRAM ADMINISTRATION AND CONFERENCE ORGANIZATION

Making a contribution that improves the quality of an academic program, committee, or other administrative endeavor.

Some academics delight in taking on administrative responsibilities, whether it be to head up an academic program, serve as the chair or member of a committee, or in some other administrative role in a department, in an institute, or in the university as a whole. Perhaps these duties represent a welcome respite from the role of instructor or researcher. In contrast, other professors may prefer to focus full-time on teaching and research. Still others may find themselves somewhere in the middle, welcoming both types of roles. Regardless, the nature of academia is such that professors are likely to find themselves in administrative roles from time to time. They may surprise themselves to see that their input to the design of an academic program or their presence on an academic committee contributes greatly to the success of this endeavor. So, regardless of whether this role fits their pictures of why they became a professor, they may derive joy from seeing that they have talents which make a difference in such undertakings.

As for me personally, I much preferred over the course of my institutional career to play a limited administrative role, focusing instead on my teaching and research. While there was undoubtedly a cost in that I did not engage in program building, there was a benefit in that my own personal career was probably more productive as a result.

Running an administrative meeting that both my colleagues and I felt was successful.

When I did serve as an administrator, I was always mindful of the criticism my colleagues tended to voice that administrative meetings were called too frequently to discuss issues of only limited importance, and that such meetings dragged on far too long. Consequently, I did my best to hold meetings infrequently and only when there were significant issues to be discussed. I tried to make sure that more minor issues were handled through electronic correspondence and other means. As for the meeting itself, I would watch the clock assiduously to ensure that the meeting dealt with the issues as expediently as possible. What a joy it would be to preside over a productive interaction among colleagues such that all in attendance were pleased with the outcome.

Having the comfort of knowing that I could return to full-time teaching and research after assuming extensive administrative duties for a period of years.

One of the advantages of academia is that when professors assume administrative duties, such as being department chair, dean of a faculty or college, assistant dean, or director of an institute, let us say, their tenure-track position is reserved for them when they cease those administrative duties. When I became head of an institute for three years at the University of Minnesota, I was fortunately able to continue to pursue some of my research activities while assuming administrative duties because a perk of my administrative role was to get an administrative assistant assigned to me. In addition, it was comforting to know that I could resume my teaching and research duties once I stepped down from the administrative ones. So not only is there a joy in job security, but there was a joy in being able to assume both instructional and administrative roles within my career as professor.

Creating a new academic center or institute and having the pleasure of seeing it gain both credibility and durability within the university community as well as within the larger community.

During the many long hours and days of deliberation that go into the planning of a new academic center or institute, there can be many moments of hesitation and doubt. What are its roles in the academic community going to be? A major concern is whether there will be adequate funding to sustain the venture. There is also the question of whether it is possible to procure the high-quality staffing necessary to make sure that this addition is a successful one in the eyes of the university community and beyond. For this reason, it gives me special joy to see a center for research and development in second-language teaching and learning at the University of Minnesota still be in existence 25 years after I helped to establish it. In fact, even though its very existence is partly determined by "soft money," the university still appears to be committed to making sure it continues to exist for many years to come, having given it an appropriate home within the institution. The center is especially known for its summer institutes, two of which I had the joy of helping to design and teach at over some years – the one on language learner styles and strategies, and the one on the teaching and learning of pragmatics. The pragmatics institute has now switched successfully to an online format over three weeks, whereas the on-site institutes are for one week.

Taking on a position of leadership within a national or international association.

There is the adage "If you want to get something done, ask a busy person." The reason that I was approached several times to run for a position as an officer in both national and international organizations was that my colleagues noticed that I liked the get things done efficiently and that I possessed leadership abilities. It was, of course, flattering to be asked to run. I had several considerations, however, about taking on such roles. On the one hand, I knew full well that my professorial duties at the time were already stretching me a bit, and that if I took on this office, I would have even more demands on my time. On the other hand, I knew that assuming such roles enhanced my annual Faculty Activity Report, since participation in national and international associations was generally looked upon favorably by my institution. In retrospect, to my satisfaction, I found that I was able to add this set of duties effectively, especially since I initially received financial support from the sponsoring association to hire a student assistant. Eventually, both the national and international associations for applied linguistics hired a professional management company, which made things easier. The joy associated with these endeavors was to find that I could acquit myself adequately in these new leadership roles, and that I was able to have some impact on the associations for which I was serving as an officer.

––––––––––––

Having my administrative knowledge sufficiently valued so that I am invited to another university to review one of their academic programs.

It is flattering for me to be invited by another university to review one of their academic programs. After all, it serves as an acknowledgment of my expertise in the field. It also provides me an opportunity to enhance the quality of a program at another university. In addition, it provides an opportunity for an inside look at how colleagues in other institutions deal with some of the same issues that I have faced at my own institutions over the years. In this case, having what I offer my colleagues be well received is a joy, and getting ideas from my colleagues to enhance my own academic experience is yet another joy.

I recently served on the three-person evaluation committee for a new M.A. program at a major institution in the Northwest. I was one of the two members of the community who participated through Skype, and this worked extremely well. I most definitely experienced the joy of both contributing and being contributed to in that the program itself was very impressive.

Organizing an academic conference that works like a dream – the speakers all have something to say and are well-received, with the discussion sessions stimulating constructive interaction.

There are lots of conferences taking place these days – perhaps even an overabundance of them. Academia has its large conventions held at convention centers in major cities. It also has an often dizzying array of smaller conferences on more specialized topics. Many of these meetings are remarkably well-attended, where in some cases attendees may have taken long train or bus rides or may have incurred flight delays and jet lag to be present. It is fair to say that expectations are usually high amongst conference goers as to the value of their attendance. Professors and graduate students may go to a number of these meetings regularly, sometimes fully paid and sometimes through institutional funding or self-funded.

One benchmark of what makes such meetings successful is the effectiveness of the keynote presentations – whether the presenters are both well-prepared and have something new and exciting to share. Another benchmark is the quality of the colloquia and the individual presentations, as well as that of the posters and book exhibits. The venue can also be important because it can be crucial to have quiet spaces in which to sit down and have a visit with a student or a colleague, perhaps for the first time or for the first time in quite a while.

A successful meeting for me is one where I come home with lots of good ideas and contacts, and where I feel motivated to follow up promptly on various notes to myself that

Andrew D. Cohen

I made at the meeting. It is one where excellent networking takes place, perhaps giving me clarity as to a new book that I may wish to write (possibly with the encouragement of editors from a publishing house), a tentative plan for new research which I wish to undertake with colleagues, and a sense that I have connected with some of my dear colleagues, many of whom are also friends.

Whether because it was my turn to host a conference, because it was my role as an officer in an association to do so, or because I simply had an epiphany that such a conference should take place, during my university career I planned numerous conferences, usually with a team of colleagues to assist me in this endeavor. We would make an effort to invite keynote speakers who were known to be highly insightful and motivational in their conference presentations. We would do our best to ensure that the presenters in colloquia and individual sessions kept to the designated time limits so as to allow extensive and fruitful discussion. In addition, we would purposely choose a given venue because it was one deemed likely to support networking among colleagues.

Both the event itself and acknowledgment received as feedback served to remind me that conferences were among the things that had attracted me to academic life in the first place. Assuming that the meeting was a successful one, I would take joy in the fact that it was satisfying for the participants, as well as for me.

———————

Planning a retreat and having the participants return to the workplace with renewed vigor.

Given that academic life can be hectic at times, it may be a real challenge to have meetings that are productive administratively and/or ones where colleagues have the time and motivation to share information about the nature of courses that they are teaching or ongoing research that they are conducting. For this reason, the solution very well may be a retreat away from the workplace. It may be just for a few hours, for a day, or even overnight. The venue need not be a long distance away, but one that is appealing, such as a cabin in the woods that ideally provides an aura of tranquility in that there are no distractions from phone calls and the like. The change of environment is intended to promote a relaxed atmosphere where both administrative and academic pursuits can take place successfully. The value of such a retreat can be huge, and when I was able to participate in such an endeavor, there was likely to be real joy associated with making it happen and having the experience of it being what was intended.

———————

Having a dinner party at my home for colleagues and students in my administrative capacity and finding it helped improve relationships.

At some points in my career – especially when I was director of an institute – I was in a position to have a dinner party at our home for colleagues and students. Whereas serving as director of an institute provided me with my fair share of encounters that were not so joyous, one of the predictably joyous undertakings for me in my role as director was to have gatherings at my home – possibly including musical

Andrew D. Cohen

entertainment furnished by students or faculty. It would provide an opportunity for interaction in an informal environment, which inevitably sparked joy for many of those involved. It was these more informal gatherings that helped to nurture relationships among those who participated, and subsequent interactions in the academic setting usually proved to be more positive as a result.

COLLEGIAL RELATIONSHIPS

Collaborating with colleagues both at my home university and at other universities nationally or internationally when the result is more powerful than it would have been had I done it on my own.

It is gratifying to know that my academic skills enable me to plan and conduct research, write papers, and give keynote addresses relying entirely on my own abilities. In fact, at times in my career, it was important for me to demonstrate what I was capable of achieving on my own as a professor in my chosen field of applied linguistics. At other times, however, the results have been far better due to collaborative efforts with colleagues. Since I am now retired, this means collaborating with colleagues at other institutions, nationally or internationally. Social media has made it easier to do this than ever before, despite the fact that if the colleague is located halfway around the world, then I must communicate (say, by Skype) either early in the morning or late at night. When this collaboration is powerful in terms of the work that the two of us are able to do jointly, then this has been a special source of joy. When the adage "Two heads are better than one" really does apply, then the results can truly be inspirational.

Receiving invaluable feedback from colleagues who are in a totally different field.

Just as it can be a joy to meet with colleagues who are in a related discipline in the spirit of interdisciplinary work and to receive feedback from their perspective, how much more stimulating and joyous it is when a meeting with a colleague from an entirely different discipline supplies me with exciting ideas for my work. Perhaps this meeting provides me with a completely new perspective that I had never considered before. An example would be when a colleague in another field is using some technology that I can readily apply to my own field as well.

***

Just knowing that I am respected by colleagues internationally.

As noted previously in this collection of joys, especially as more colleagues and students get successfully hooked up to the Internet both on their own equipment and through institutions, an academic's visibility is likely to grow. Academic websites like ResearchGate and Academia have served important networking roles in getting colleagues connected worldwide. One outcome of this enhanced international visibility is that I personally feel more connected with colleagues around the world than ever before.

Collegial support for my work has shown up as their responding to questionnaires that I have sent out, sharing their most recent work with me at my request, or agreeing to present their work in a colloquium.

Students around the world will email me requesting assistance with their research, especially those living in countries where they have more limited access to academic

Andrew D. Cohen

work through their own institutions, and where contacting me provides them a form of lifeline to what is currently happening in the field.

This sense of connectedness and the tangible rewards from it have most certainly brought me joy.

Contributing in a significant way to the thinking and output of my colleagues – for example, seeing colleagues get their ideas into print, thanks in part to my guidance and support.

On numerous occasions over the years, I have found myself in a coaching role, especially with more junior colleagues. For example, I served as mentor to numerous visiting scholars who came to the University of Minnesota. They were predominantly from China. In other cases, my guidance and support have been through chains of email messages which include papers and reports that I have attached to them or have made available to them on my personal website (z.umn.edu/adcohen). Over the years, I have posted whatever of my writings publishers grant me rights to put on my personal website, along with PowerPoint presentations and descriptions of my current projects.

It is often with joy, then, that I witness these colleagues successfully getting their work published. I know from my behind-the-scenes work with them that my interventions have had some impact both on the way they have thought about and have addressed the issues and on how they have written about them. Often I have given them feedback on several drafts of their papers. While I have rarely gotten remunerated for the guidance I have provided, I have had the satisfaction of knowing that I have played a crucial role in supporting other colleagues in their academic efforts.

The excitement when a discussion with a colleague or colleagues really contributes to my thinking on a given academic topic of interest to me, perhaps opening up a new area of academic pursuit.

My thinking about major topics of interest to me has been formulated over a series of years. Even in areas where I consider myself open-minded about the issues, my stance is still likely to be relatively set. So, it can be a joy to have the outcome of a discussion with colleagues lead me to question my own thinking about an academic topic. The discussion may have triggered a new direction for my thinking and writing, and possibly even a new line of research. In other career areas, especially in the business world, tasks at work may be assigned by superiors, whereas in academia, professors usually have the joy of crafting their own areas of thought and research. In fact, a department may be delighted to see academics expanding their foci of interest and investigation. The joy for me in my career has been in taking on a new and highly stimulating line of thought and investigation, just at a time when I was perhaps overly entrenched in certain ways of thinking about issues.

Having the joy of being sincerely recognized by my colleagues in the written acknowledgments that they include in their publications.

As I mentioned above, there are many behind-the-scenes ways that professors can support their colleagues in their efforts to publish their written work. Colleagues may have approached me asking me what I have done recently in such and such an area and I have sent them along an email response or two, including as attachments some of my recent papers. They may have sent me a draft of a paper that they are writing. They might simply be sharing their ideas which they are still formulating. Given how I have perceived my role as an academic in the field, I usually find time to pause in my own work to support that of my colleagues. So, when my colleagues' work is published and they include in their acknowledgments recognition of my contribution to them, I experience a moment of joy.

Working closely with colleagues over the years, gaining their trust and respect and coming to trust and respect them, such that they also become good friends.

Some of the colleagues that I interact with regularly and those that I have come to know and admire nationally and throughout the world also become my good friends. It is not so surprising when I consider that these are people with whom I have shared scrumptious meals at lovely restaurants, gone sightseeing with as time has permitted around the academic program at conferences, shared coffee breaks with at numerous meetings, and have often been in regular contact with through emails. I have come to know a lot about them and their families, and thus not so surprisingly I feel connected with them. They may even have given me a house gift one of the times that they came to dinner which has become one of my prized possessions. With the advent of social media, we usually acknowledge birthdays regularly and are aware of other meaningful events in each other's lives. Out of these relatively frequent contacts, we have developed a level of mutual trust and respect that is endearing, and so constitutes a key joy associated with my being a professor.

Finding out that my professional friends are true friends at a time of personal need.

As much as I value my collegial relationships which are renewed at our annual meetings, I am still surprised to see how deeply colleagues really do care about me at moments of need, such as when I lose a dear family member or when I myself am going through a health crisis. These colleagues may be there for me. It may be that I am walking or running for some particular cause and they are quick to make a contribution to that cause. It is especially heartwarming because these are people with whom my face-to-face interactions are usually limited to once-a-year basis at best. The joy is in experiencing just how deep the friendship actually is, despite its seemingly intermittent nature.

TENURE, ACADEMIC FREEDOM, AND THE ACADEMIC CALENDAR

Having freedom to decide what to include in a course that I am teaching.

Whereas the institute, department, or program in which I taught during my professorial career occasionally specified certain courses that I was expected to offer, I still had a good deal of freedom with regard to what I chose to include within each of these designated courses. For example, I always had free reign over the topics that were covered in a given course, the assigned and recommended readings, the assignments that students were asked to complete, the nature of the assessment procedures, and a host of other issues. In addition to these courses, I also offered a number of courses and seminars that I myself developed from scratch – beyond the basic curriculum. I also had freedom regarding just how I organized my courses – e.g. the decisions I made about what would happen when during the semester or quarter, how a given class session would unfold, and so forth.

Certainly, having so many choices can be mind-boggling, but on the other hand I viewed it as an opportunity for me to let my creative juices flow as a professor. This was a source of joy for me over the years. While teaching at the Hebrew University of Jerusalem in Israel, I even had the freedom to determine whether I would teach a course for a semester or for an entire year, which included the liberty to designate a period of months in a research seminar where there would not be class sessions at all in order to give my graduate students time to do field research.

Being able to select as research projects only those topics which really motivate me.

The opposite of joy when it comes to doing research is when professors find themselves doing a study that is singularly unmotivating for whatever reason. It may have been a study that from the get-go they were not committed to but felt an obligation to undertake, whether alone or with colleagues. In contrast, conducting a study when fully engaged and eager to see the findings unfold can be a highly motivating experience, and commensurately a source of joy. It may be a topic that I have wanted to research for some time and finally have an opportunity to do so. It may be that I have just received a grant that makes it possible to conduct the study with the new resources that I have been provided, or a colleague of mine has the time and energy to collaborate with me on it – willingly taking on the tasks that I would have needed to hire an assistant to conduct. Whatever the circumstances may be, being fully committed to conducting a particular study can make it a highly joyful experience.

Having job security through the tenure system.

Although professors may have had to jump through many hoops to get tenure, once they have it they are most likely not in imminent danger of being terminated – unless, of course, they have committed some egregious infraction. True, to receive promotions and pay increases, they may need to demonstrate regularly that their work is progressing nicely in keeping with departmental and university-wide standards. They may well need to prepare an annual faculty activity report in which they list their publications for the year, as well as any instructional accomplishments and administrative activities. The good thing is that while this report provides a benchmark of academic activity over the years, it is usually not used as a justification for terminating employment at the given institution. Given that people in other professions may well be let go at a moment's notice, the academic profession provides an admirable level of job security, which is a joy.

———————

Having a block of time in the summer to catch up on all those projects that the academic year provided little time to deal with, as well as to have quality vacation time.

Professors may have a mother-in-law or some other family member who has commented more than once on the fact that being a professor is a cushy job since during the summer months there is no mandatory teaching. Professors know that the summer months provide a most welcome safety net. This is a time which I looked forward to each year to do the readings and course preparation that were essential for me in making my instructional offerings valuable to my students. In addition, at times it was during the summer that I would engage in research projects that I did not have the time for when I was busy teaching. Summers breaks were crucial for me as well in that they provided an opportunity to have quality time with family and friends.

So, there was most definitely a joy associated with the advent of the summer months each year. Now in semi-retirement, I must admit that I pay less attention to the seasons and how they relate to academic semesters. That too is a joy – not having to be concerned anymore about what used to be crucial benchmarks for me in my career.

Having those days in the week or periods during the year when I can plan my work schedule largely the way I want to.

What a true joy it can be to determine, at least to some extent, the nature of my work schedule such that I can plan when I start each day and when I finish – so that I can schedule in other activities as well, such as sports, music, family events, or whatever. Unlike employment in other types of work where my schedule is largely or fully determined by my superiors, I had the good fortune over the years to have academic positions where I could craft my own personal work schedule – one that functioned for me in that it accommodated all my academic responsibilities, as well as my own personal needs that included time with family. Before retirement, being a professor entailed juggling a lot of different responsibilities effectively, along with my regular sports activities which meant playing on university squash teams for many years, as well as cycling to and from work. Hence, being able to devise a work schedule that made everything happen just the way I wanted it was a joy.

Being paid a good salary for doing what I really wanted to do anyway.

When I was growing up, I remember having the notion that in order to obtain a substantial salary, it was likely that I would need to take on a fair number of tasks that would not be appealing to me in order to get compensated. What a joy then to arrive at a point where my professorial salary would be considered "good" by national standards, perhaps thanks to various salary bumps along the way – for academic accomplishments, as well as for administrative duties performed. The joy came with the realization that this decent salary was being paid to me for doing what I really wanted to do anyway.

Having a job that provides for sabbatical leaves, and then taking one or more where I am truly freed from all of my regular duties.

One of the super joys of being a professor is when my institution afforded me unfettered sabbatical time to go off and do "my thing" anywhere in the world for a year. Over my career, I took four such sabbaticals – the first being from Israel back to my former institution, UCLA (1980-81), the second being from Israel to the Pontifical Catholic University in São Paolo, Brazil (1986-87), the third being from Minneapolis to the University of Hawaii in Honolulu and then on to Tel Aviv University in Israel (1996-97), and the fourth being from Minneapolis to Auckland University in

New Zealand (2004-5).

I have colleagues who, for a number of reasons, have chosen to spend their sabbaticals at home, where almost inadvertently they find themselves engaged in university business when they are ostensibly on leave. In my case, however, I was able to take sabbatical leaves far from my institution for a full 12 months. Not only was I freed from my regular academic duties, but I had the joy of experiencing academic life in another part of the world and with other standards for how things were done.

When my sabbatical was in country that abided by the tradition of having a mandatory coffee/tea break every morning from 10 to 10:30 AM in a faculty lounge – as in New Zealand – then I had the joy of fraternizing with colleagues on a daily basis to compare notes about our lives and to celebrate birthdays and other occasions as they arose during the year. In the helter-skelter academic world in numerous countries, academic schedules are often crafted such that faculty do not have their breaks at the same time, except for the slot for faculty meetings that are not usually intended for fraternizing. So, a huge part of the joy can be a result of the change of venue and all that it brings with it, including fostering long-term ties with colleagues.

TECHNOLOGY

Having my institution provide me a new computer that was faster and more efficient than the one I had, and having tech support.

The image below purposely shows a hugely outdated computer, one that used to take up a good deal of desk space. Now computers come with flat screens, often with the hard drive in the back of the screen, rather than in a separate tower or box.

It made me feel very supported when the University of Minnesota provided me on a regular basis state-of-the-art computers – both desktops and laptops – for my computing needs during the 22 years that I worked there. In the early years, tech support meant coming to my office and working on the computer problem directly before it morphed into remote access. I also received either free of charge or at a minimal cost software programs essential for my work as a professor, whereas in the past I had had to purchase them, sometimes at great expense.

The perk of being fully supported in my computational needs has been a tremendous source of joy. I would add that in retirement I still receive complimentary updated versions of Microsoft Office, as well as 24/7 support from the Technology Helpline at the University of Minnesota. That is a joy.

**Becoming so knowledgeable about a software
program that I find myself giving guidance on
its use to students and fellow colleagues.**

Not knowing how a software program works can be frustrating, especially when it is necessary to have facility with this program to collect data in a highly specialized way, conduct crucial analyses of data, or design and deliver a presentation. Contrast this with the satisfaction that I have gotten when I know the ins and outs of the program, perhaps after hours of pouring over the software manual (now largely replaced by simply doing a Google search) or

Andrew D. Cohen

after repeated use of the trial-and-error approach.

I have now reached a point where I am relatively knowledgeable about how to use Microsoft Word, PowerPoint, and certain other programs, such as Survey Monkey. It has been a joy over my career to have gone from limited or no knowledge to being the resident expert on a given software program. I have experienced this joy, especially as it pertained to the analysis of data from language tests, as I had my students in a language assessment class that I taught regularly analyze the results of the tests that they had constructed.

Having a colleague who knows more than I do about some new software walk me through how to use it properly.

Just as it can be a joy to be the resident expert on some software, it can also be a joy to not be an expert at all, but rather to have easy access to a colleague who not only is an expert on that software, but who is also highly accessible to me and always ready to give me assistance with it. As a professor, I am called upon to be an expert in many areas. Consequently, it can be a delight to have some areas where I can revel in my ignorance, knowing that others will provide me the assistance I need to get the job done.

Having a colleague come to me with a computer problem that I can solve.

While I never envisioned myself an expert when it came to computers and computing, the longer I have been in the field the more I have become aware that users differ in computer skills. At one end there are people who are challenged by the basics and at the other end there are experts who can engage in multitasking on multiple screens in ways that boggle my mind. I consider myself somewhere in the middle. The joy here comes in discovering that I know a bit more than some colleague about some software such as Microsoft Word, PowerPoint, or a program for statistical analysis such as SPSS, and am therefore able to assist this colleague in resolving a computer issue.

Discovering a software program that does just what is needed and then having the joy of using it successfully.

It is well-known that the intention of computer software is usually to assist us in handling tasks more efficiently than without the use of such a program. Since I have been in the field a long time, I distinctly remember when there was no such program to facilitate my completion of a given task, such as providing a subject and author index for a book. So, it was a joyful experience for me to use a software program that created subject and author indices instantly, allowing me to focus my time on the categorization and sub-categorization of entries, and not on tabulating the page numbers. The program did it quickly and efficiently, which was a genuine relief for me. Not only was it a joy at the time, but it is also a joy now every time I use these 18 pages of indices (!). Needless to say, the subject index is anything but perfunctory; it is substantive – which makes it more informative about the book, thanks to the computer program that assisted me in its creation.

Using the Review mode in Word for making comments on students' and colleagues' papers, articles, and chapters.

Professors who have been in the field for many years remember the days before students wrote their papers and submitted them electronically – the days when papers were submitted on a hardcopy basis and professors were expected to scribble marginal comments on these papers. The advent of electronic submissions and of software that allows reviewers to make comments in boxes at the margin has revolutionized professor-student communication. Add to this then the possibility of using a voice recognition program and professors can now use marginal notes as a highly efficient means to provide ongoing commentary while reading a student's or colleague's paper. Especially if a professor's handwriting is not so legible when trying to write quickly, having the comments produced digitally removes the handwriting issue altogether. I have also found that I am more inclined to offer lengthier and more rigorous comments given this greater that process of providing comments as now been made easier.

The digital era has also greatly facilitated the process whereby students submit their work to professors. Again, those in the field for many years remember when students submitted handwritten papers, especially in countries where typing was considered a menial undertaking and where students could not afford to have professional typists do the final version of their papers. All of this is a thing of the past. Hence, there are multiple joys in both receiving legible papers from students and in being able to provide students ample and legible feedback.

Finding that I get the perfect solution to a computer issue by doing a Google search, rather than hunting for it in a technical manual.

It used to be the case that resolving some computer issue involved spending a good deal of time trying to find the answer in a technical manual, and finding that this manual was not well written (possibly a translation from some other language) and perhaps was even out of date, so that it did not provide a solution for the problem at hand. Contrast this with the current situation whereby I can simply ask my question in a Google search and have a series of possible solutions pop up on my screen, one of which actually does resolve the issue. It may even be accompanied by a YouTube video clip in which some knowledgeable person walks me through the steps and shows me on the screen just what happens at each interval. This current reality has been a source of great joy, especially if the computer glitch had caused me endless frustration up to the point where I realized that it was a solvable problem and that I could use Google to look for a solution.

BUILDING MY
PROFESSIONAL LIBRARY

Receiving pre-publication versions of books and papers which help to give me that comfortable feeling that I am up-to-date in the field.

For the sake of my credibility as a scholar in my academic field, it is important for me to stay abreast of recent developments in the literature, either because certain new publications can benefit my current thinking about issues in the field or my teaching about them, or can inform the research in which I am engaged. It might also be that these publications cite the work of other scholars which is beneficial to me. Yet, at a time when there is a proliferation of journals worldwide, as well as increasing numbers of publishing houses, keeping on top of the literature is a challenge. The act of reviewing submissions for publication to journals serves to remind me about the consequences of being out of date. It may, in fact, be the case that a given study that I am reviewing is based on theories in the literature which have been superseded by other theories in the more up-to-date literature. The research instruments and the means for data collection may also be out-of-date.

Whereas in the past, it might have been possible to track publications in what were then the key journals or book series, in today's academic world this is easier said than done. So I have found that I have needed to be a bit proactive by contacting key colleagues, checking with publishers about their forthcoming volumes, and the like. The outcome of these efforts may be that I have received pre-publication versions of books and papers which have helped me to be up-to-date in the field. Publishers sometimes ask me to review a proposal for a new book or to evaluate the draft of a new book. This is also a way to find out about what is new and upcoming in the field. Having a sense that I am aware of the most recent literature on topics of concern to me in the field can be a true source of joy.

Receiving complimentary copies of published papers or books from my colleagues.

It can be a super joy when my colleagues send me a hot-off-the-press printed or digital version of their new book or attach to me a new article of theirs, especially if I was unaware that this publication was in the works. Such an event simply reminds me of how fortunate I am to be so connected with colleagues in the field, some of them remarkably prolific.

Having publishers invite me to select copies of key books in my field as a courtesy to me for reviewing book proposals or books.

Whereas in the distant past publishers sometimes sent me copies of books simply as an acknowledgment of my status in the field or in response to advice that I had provided them as to possible authors for books in their various series, nowadays it is more likely that I am invited to select books in my field as recompense for evaluations that I have done for them. At times, the reading of one of these books has opened up new vistas for me in my own thinking and development. So, instead of having to go to the library to hunt for books, publishers have been alerting me to their latest offerings and making them readily available to me, which is, in itself, a major joy since there is usually some delay before new books are received and then cataloged for circulation in university libraries. In addition, digital copies of these academic books (my preference these days) may be unavailable in the university libraries.

_____

Being given a university stipend or grant money to purchase books that I needed in order to enhance my collection of significant volumes in the fields of interest to me.

At times there have been books that I really wanted to have access to, whether because the books were not yet available in my university library or because I needed to refer to them during an extended period of time. In such cases, it was a great joy to receive a university stipend through an award or grant money that allowed me to purchase these desired volumes at no cost to myself.

_____

Being able to loan a student some crucial book that the university library does not have.

At times my personal academic library ended up being a vital asset in my efforts to assist my students when they were in need of books crucial to them for the design of a research project, for a course paper, or whatever. Although this would put me in the role of librarian, on numerous occasions it would also be a source of joy to know that the valuable collection I had amassed could be of timely benefit to those that I served in my academic community.

Building a digital library just when my shelf space is so limited that I do not know what I would do with more physical books.

Whereas perhaps unimaginable in the past and still resisted by those who prefer a printed book in their hands, I have found it a joy to amass a digital library. The main reason is that in our relatively small retirement condominium, I do not have shelf space to store new books. In addition, digital access usually allows me to find and cite my sources more expeditiously. While it is true that having books physically on a shelf makes them more visible in some ways, I do keep an electronic listing of my digital books and update it as I get new acquisitions. A digital library may have been futuristic in the past, but now it is a tangible reality. It can be a joy to be reaping the benefits of such a digital library.

CORRESPONDENCE

Having emailing facilitate my daily correspondence – in getting messages and attachments out both nationally and internationally.

As long as I am careful before pushing the "send" button to make sure that I have not sent some message that I will later regret having sent, emailing has facilitated my professorial act tremendously. Professors who were engaged in academic life before email attachments will remember how frustrating it was sometimes to be dependent on conventional mail delivery and even expedited delivery. They may also remember those cases where some crucial mail was sent to the wrong address, while with emailing there is often instant notification when a message has been sent to an undeliverable address.

Years ago, I would disseminate my academic papers to colleagues either using a stencil or ditto machine or more recently Xerox machines. Whichever processes are used – and the former ones were messy – I then had to collate the pages, find mailing envelopes for all of the papers, properly address them, and then send them in the mail, with the mailroom sometimes giving me flack for the amount of postage this entailed, depending on how long the list of recipients was. Now the document is attached electronically in a jiffy and sent off to colleagues and students. It may also be posted on a personal website or some website for academics.

The writing or editing of books with the constant back-

and-forth among colleagues and publishers has never been easier than it is now. One can only imagine what future technologies will present themselves that will make academic communication still easier.

Especially those who remember how challenging it used to be to disseminate academic work in the past will undoubtedly share in the joy that I derive from the way it now is.

――――――――

Getting a special email message that really makes my day.

When I open my email in the morning, I am never quite sure just what my list of messages will include. Hopefully the number of undesired messages that get through my University of Minnesota firewall are now reduced to a minimum. When I was engaged in active instruction, I always received emails from students, often with requests that I do something for them right away. What can be a source of joy is to get really special email messages that make my day, such as when a paper is accepted for publication, a book I have written has been given an excellent review and a colleague or the publisher have passed this on to me, or I have been acknowledged for some special contribution that I made in a colleague or student's life. Since a certain amount of my emailing could be referred to as "perfunctory," these really special messages definitely stand out from the other messages so much so that they put a smile on my face and help to make my day or week, depending.

Finding out that a recommendation letter I wrote was instrumental in a student or colleague's obtaining a job, tenure, a promotion, a grant, or an award.

As a professor, I often find myself in a position where a timely letter from me can be instrumental in a student or colleague's efforts to get a job, tenure, a promotion, a grant, or an award. Consequently, I take these assignments seriously and usually invest a good deal of time and effort in making sure that such letters are well thought out and will be persuasive. Given my many years of experience in writing such letters, I have learned how to craft them with certain choice phrases intended to make it difficult for the recipients not to take my input seriously. It is nonetheless a continual source of joy to hear from the given student or colleague that my letter was instrumental in their obtaining what it is that they were seeking. This happy outcome serves as a reminder of ways that I have contributed to the lives of others around me in my role as professor over the years.

Getting a "thank you" note from students or colleagues acknowledging me for the letter of recommendation I wrote, the administrative task I assumed, or the contribution my teaching made in their lives.

As a professor I have taken on many duties and often without even a second thought. I have simply considered it part of what is expected of a university professor. But every so often those who were recipients of my intervention on their behalf are motivated to give me significant positive feedback in acknowledgment of what I did for them. What may heighten the joy associated with this feedback is that I was not expecting any such feedback since in my mind I was simply doing my job. Whatever the specific situation entailed, the joy is sparked in part by the element of surprise, as well as by the reminder it brings me that others are grateful for the contribution that I made to them.

Andrew D. Cohen

GRANTS, AWARDS, AND OTHER FORMS OF ACKNOWLEDGMENT

Receiving a grant – whether large or small – for teaching, research, or travel.

Some decades ago it was relatively common for university departments to have a travel allotment included in their annual budget so that professors could travel to conferences of importance to them in their academic fields. Also, these budget stipends might have included financial support for teaching and research projects as well. In addition, there were numerous non-university sources for funding of research studies. It is probably fair to say that departmental budgets in the Humanities and Social Sciences no longer provide funding for these areas.

Nowadays, stipends for travel, research, and teaching projects are likely to be obtainable primarily through grants that the recipients need to have applied for, and where competition is high – often university-wide.

Hence, my receipt of such grants in the final years of my career was most definitely a source of joy since it provided me the financial means to support timely research in my field, to travel to a conference or two in order to present what I deemed a valuable contribution, to plan and then carry out the detailed work essential for the creation of a new course that I wanted to teach, or to design a website.

Receiving a major acknowledgment for scholarship, teaching, or service to the field.

Given the large number of faculty members at any given university these days, it may not be a given that a professor will be acknowledged for scholarship, teaching, or administrative contributions. All the more reason then for me to feel joy when I received an award from the College of Liberal Arts at the University of Minnesota as "Scholar of the College." I remember that I needed to provide documentation of my case to a colleague who then submitted it, but given the competition, I did not expect to be an awardee. Hence, receiving such an award was a pleasant surprise. Three professors out of several hundred received the award annually, and it came with a three-year financial stipend.

Being acknowledged in the form of a picture and article about me appearing in a university newspaper or magazine, or in the popular press.

It can be special to be singled out in the media of one's institution, in the local press, or in the international press for some accomplishment in the academic arena – whether it be for teaching, research, or administrative innovations. I have had such media coverage from time to time. Most recently I was contacted by a South American journalist covering the World Cup in Russia. He wanted to know my views on the extensive use of Google Translate at that time. My response appeared in the international press – the Associated Press and the New York Times, as well as in other news outlets. Each time I am quoted or references made to my academic contributions in the press at whatever level, it is unquestionably a source of joy.

Basking in the glory of receiving "professorship" in an academic community where the title "professor" is clearly an important step up from "doctor."

Professors who have arrived at the title of "full professor" are undoubtedly aware of what it took for them to arrive at this status. It may well have entailed a drawn out and often arduous process. It may be all the more valued if they are working within an academic system where the title "professor" is reserved exclusively for those who have risen to this status on the basis of publication record, research achievements, exemplary teaching, and the like. Hence, when the title of professor was conferred upon me at the Hebrew University in Jerusalem, this was truly a joyous moment where I felt that I had finally reached the status of professor.

Getting a royalty statement on a book and seeing that more people than I had expected have purchased the volume.

Unlike stage actors who get to see the turnout for a given play that they are acting in, professors when they write academic works often have little sense of how many people are accessing their writing. So, royalties for publications can be one yardstick of success in the field. This obviously is only one yardstick since many readers may access publications through their local institutional libraries. Others may get access to excerpts from Google Docs. Still, a royalty statement gives some sense of success, particularly when book prices keep rising.

It is true that royalties are not just for books, but can also be for rights to reprint passages from my writings or the full text, given that there are entities which collect up royalties and provide them on a semi-annual basis. I am also receiving royalties from an online course on language assessment that I wrote some years ago and for which I provided a dozen video clips.

Given that applied linguistics is not a highly lucrative field like medicine, engineering, or law, every bit of income accrued is appreciated. Hence, regular royalty payments produce joy. It is more the principle of the thing then a matter of gaining wealth. Once I accidentally got a six-month royalty statement for a co-author of a high school math textbook. It was for $24,000, reminding me that I had not chosen a particularly lucrative field – at least with respect to royalties for publications, but nonetheless mine is a field that I have found over the years to be most engaging.

Continuing to get reasonable royalty checks for a book that was written some years ago.

It is a special type of joy to find that a book which I wrote over a decade ago is being purchased in numbers that still provide royalty income. What makes this joy so unique is that I may well not have this publication on my radar screen anymore. It is an indicator that my work has stood the test of time. Having this insight about my work is itself a source of joy.

Getting a raise based on merit, namely, my talks, publications, and service to my academic department and to the field.

During my years in Israel, my salary was fixed at my particular professorial level regardless of my performance as a Senior Lecturer and then as an Associate Professor. This was certainly not the case when I returned to the US and found that my pay was determined largely by what I accomplished. While I did not receive an endowed chair during my career as a professor in the US, my academic endeavors were sufficient to procure me a series of raises based on merit (as opposed to an equity raise which was intended to keep my salary at par with the cost-of-living). It was especially pleasing to me since I received the merit increase because I regularly accepted invitations to give talks at notable conferences, to write publications for respectable venues, and to serve in administrative roles requiring leadership skills at my local institution as well as in national or international associations in my field. The joy came from knowing that I definitely earned the merit increase.

Having my children recognize me not only as a parent but also as a teacher and a scholar, as they have direct or indirect contact with my students and my colleagues in my field.

For professors with children, the children are most likely to see their parents first and foremost in the parental role.

At times, being a professor means having to take numerous trips to academic meetings, coming home late in the evening due to academic events or perhaps sports activities (a crucial way to offset academic pressures), and working at home in order to make certain deadlines.

Telling my children about my accomplishments in my field would not have been a very cool thing to do. So, a neat way for them to find this out was from my students and colleagues, when they would share with my daughter and son flattering things about me, including anecdotes about me that helped my children appreciate me more in terms of my professorial contributions to the field. If the truth be told, I did want my children to respect me for my track record as a professor, especially since some of my time spent in professorial pursuits meant that I was less engaged in their lives than I would have wished to be.

While my children may have wanted me to spend more time with them – especially in the early years, it has been a joy to see as they get older the pride that they take in my professorial accomplishments. I have also had the joy of watching my daughter and son develop into consummate professionals, both highly skilled in what they have undertaken, with daughter Judy being in a tenure-track position as a college instructor in theater and art for disabled adults and son Daniel being high up in the corporate structure in the business world. Both of them are most articulate in speaking to groups, and it brings joy to me to suppose that the model they received from their father as a public speaker contributed to their own professional act.

ABOUT THE AUTHOR

Andrew D. Cohen was a Peace Corps Volunteer on the High Plains of Bolivia (1965-67) working in community development with the Aymara Indians, taught in the ESL Section of the English Department at UCLA for four years, and was Professor of Language Education at the School of Education, Hebrew University of Jerusalem (1975-1991) during which time he served as a Fulbright Lecturer/Researcher in Applied Linguistics to Brazil (1986-87). From 1991 to 2013, he was Professor of Second Language Studies at the University of Minnesota, Minneapolis. During his Minnesota years, he was a Visiting Scholar at the University of Hawaii (1996-7) and at Tel Aviv University (1997), and a Visiting Lecturer at Auckland University in New Zealand (2004-5). He is now Professor Emeritus from the University of Minnesota, and lives with his wife of 50 years, Sabina, in Oakland, CA. Their son and daughter each have three children, so they are proud grandparents of six.

He is co-editor of *Language learning strategies* with Ernesto Macaro (Oxford University Press, 2007), author of *Strategies in learning and using a second language* (Routledge, 2011), co-author of *Teaching and learning pragmatics* with Noriko Ishihara (Routledge, 2014, which has been translated into Japanese and Arabic, and a Korean translation is currently in the works), and most recently author of *Learning pragmatics from native and nonnative language teachers* (Multilingual Matters, 2018). He has also authored many book chapters and journal articles. A number of his publications are available on his personal website: https://z. umn.edu/adcohen.

Cohen is now semi-retired and continues to engage in research, to present at national and international conferences, to publish his writings, to study Chinese largely in order to stay in touch with the language acquisition process, and to take on various professorial activities that he finds appealing. Needless to say, the joys of being a professor still pervade his life.

His non-professorial pursuits include playing trumpet in a community band, playing guitar for group singing, cycling around Oakland and Berkeley on both a bicycle and a tricycle, working out regularly at the YMCA, playing with his Oakland- and Florida-based grandchildren within limits given his MS, going to theatrical performances and concerts, watching movies and sitcoms with his spouse, and reading popular books for discussion in his men's book club.

Made in the USA
Monee, IL
28 August 2020